CHRISTIAN AMERICAN PARTY

ROGER H. EWING

CHRISTIAN AMERICAN PARTY
Copyright © 2015 by Roger H. Ewing

ISBN-13: 978-1511473149
ISBN-10: 1511473142

Printed in the United States of America
Formatting provided by Manuscripts To Go/Book & Manuscripts Services

Other Published Books

"BOMBING AMERICA, The Deception of the American
People" Published October 1, 2014

"Solving America's Debt and Deficit"
Published in May 2011

"It is Written -- the Shocking Downfall of the USA"
Published in November 2009

"Powerful Guide to Living the Good Life"
Published in December 1998
An Inspirational book

Subject of Master's Thesis:
"How to Solve a Problem"
Received an A+ from the University of Southern California
in 1970

CONTENTS

THE CHRISTIAN AMERICAN PARTY

J esus said, "If you deny me before man, I will deny you before my Father who is in heaven". That's on Judgment Day! We are to not only accept Jesus Christ as our Lord and Savior, but to live a Christian life.

The Bible states that we, you and I, are either with God or we, you and I, are against God. It is our, yours and mine, choice to make for all eternity. There is no middle ground. We, you and I, are either all 100% in or we, you and I, are out. I have made my choice, I am 100% with Jesus Christ, the Son, and God, the Father.

This is YOUR moment to make the decision if you are with Jesus Christ and God. If YOU are 100% in with Jesus Christ and God then NOW it's time to support a political party that has as its foundation the Word of God. If YOU believe in God's principles you need to stand with the newly formed CHRISTIAN AMERICAN PARTY. Join us as we return the United States of America back into a Christian nation.

WHAT WE BELIEVE. We believe Jesus Christ is the Son of God. We believe Jesus Christ came to earth to save us from our sins. We believe in the virgin birth. We believe Jesus was perfect. He died for anyone who believes in Him as our Savior and Lord and as a new born again Christian we strive to live according to the Bible principles.

WHAT WE STAND FOR

1. The Bible and the Ten Commandments
2. The Bill of Rights
3. The Constitution of the United States of America.
4. We the People

WHAT WE STAND FOR

1. The first priority of the President and Congress of the United States of America is NATIONAL DEFENSE. This includes BORDER SECURITY ALL AROUND OUR NATION, A STRONG MILITARY AND STRONG SUPPORT FOR OUR VETERANS (ACTIVE AND RETIRED). Support Israel. Find a legal way to reduce the power of the office of the President. It's been proven the U.S. Congress is not up to the job of their power of the purse. Foreign policy is to defeat evil.

2. A strong economy led by middle class jobs. A return to a strong private manufacturing sector. A return of thousands of jobs that went overseas to China and other foreign countries. Analyze all of

our international trade treaties. Reduce and eliminate the 18 trillion dollar debt.

3. Limited federal government. A reduction of the ever growing federal bureaucracy. Return to Constitutional government. Return to Rule of Law. Congressional accountability. Eliminate wasteful federal government spending using as a starter Senator Coburn's report. Congressional term limits.

4. The Supreme Court, federal courts, and state courts. The courts have NO AUTHORITY to make laws or to change laws The U.S. Congress and state legislatures make laws. Three examples of Supreme Court rulings that changed the law. Roe vs. Wade. Over 50 million babies have been killed by abortion since Roe vs. Wade, Everson vs. Board of Education. This decision separated the church and state. We need to restore religion to its proper place, another Supreme Court decision based on a phrase in a letter by Thomas Jefferson to a friend that had no standing or legality, and the Affordable Care Act (Obamacare), another Supreme Court decision changing the word "penalty" to "taxes". We need term limits for Supreme Court justices.

5. Pro Life and Private property rights.

6. Foreign Aid. Analyze all foreign aid. Eliminate foreign aid to countries who oppose us.

7. United Nations. We fund somewhere between 50% to 65% for the operations of the UN. No one knows for sure how much we contribute. We need to investigate our role and expenditures for the UN.

8. Audit the Federal Reserve Bank. Take appropriate action to reduce their influence.

9. 10th Amendment. Return rights to states that the federal government has confiscated.

10. Reform the tax code. Reform the IRS.

11. Energy policy. Eliminate attack on the coal industry. Do independent study on heavily subsidized wind energy where millions of dollars have been wasted.

12. Immigration. First secure the borders. Enforce existing immigration laws. Develop an immigration policy that finally will work.

For anyone who is interested in helping this author in this mammoth undertaking, your help will be greatly appreciated. The odds are against achieving success. Here is one of my life slogans. "I have had success, and I have had failure, but the ONLY real failure is in NOT trying".

You know we need to accomplish the goal. The goal is worthy of your effort. There is a great deal of work ahead. America needs a political party that will listen to the people after they have overwhelming voted against the liberal takeover of our country and both parties are complicit. You have probably said to yourself that we need a third party that will stand up for "WE THE PEOPLE" Here is your chance. Get involved!

HERE IS WHAT WE HAVE TO DO

1. Call your Secretary of State's office. Ask them what the requirements are to getting a new political party recognized by your state.

2. Ask them how to get a new political party on the ballot in your state. They will likely tell you to get a petition. Have them send you one.

3. The petition will require you to get signatures of people in your state. Every state is different to the number of signatures needed to get on the ballot.

4. There is a deadline to getting the signatures.

5. Most likely you will need help in getting the signatures. A suggestion is to send out a press

release to the news media in your area to inform people of what we are doing. Also, you may want to have a meeting to explain to interested people what we are doing. You may want to have a meeting in several cities in your state. Try to involve as many people who are willing to work to meet our goals. This is a grass roots effort of "We the People".

6. Please keep me informed of your progress. If you need any help please let me know ASAP. You can send me an email at amcapparty@aol.com and put CAP in the subject line. CAP stands for Christian American Party. CAP could also mean it's time to put a CAP on the abusive powers of the DEMOCRATIC AND REPUBLICAN PARTIES.

7. Each state should elect a Chairman or Chairwoman to be the leader of the Christian American Party. It is suggested that a Board of Advisors be elected to work hand in hand with the Chairperson. Depending on the population of your state it would probably be in your best interests to elect people from around the state and not just from one community.

8. Once you have secured the signatures needed for your state you and the people who have helped, will need to find a qualified candidate to run for the United States Senate, the U.S. House of Representatives, your state house, and local

elections. This author is working on getting a nationally known qualified candidate to run for President. Again, each state is different. Some states may require you have a list of candidates running for the offices mentioned and some MAY only require you have a candidate for President. Check with your Secretary of State's office.

THE ONLY REASON THAT THE AUTHOR NEEDS TO TRY TO GET A NATIONALLY KNOWN PERSON TO BE THE PRESIDENTIAL CANDIDATE IS BECAUSE OF THE TIME IT WILL TAKE TO GET ALL 50 STATES RECOGNIZED BY THEIR RESPECTIVE STATES. THERE WILL NOT BE MUCH TIME TO HAVE A CONVENTION AND THEN HAVE OUR CANDIDATE CAMPAIGN ALL OVER THE COUNTRY.

9. Reality is that we will need donations. We will need the donations to get the word out what we are doing. We will need donations to help our candidates get elected because we need to advertise on their behalf. The author is working to find an organization that will handle the donations. Please email the author if you want to donate at amcapparty@aol.com. as the book needs to go to the publisher. Your donations are vital for our success, please email the author for further information on where to send donations.

IT IS WRITTEN that we need to live in God's word. What does that mean? God's word is outlined in the Bible. In order to believe God's word one must believe the Bible is the inspired word of God. That God inspired the authors' of the Bible to write exactly what God wanted we the people to know. We must in faith need to read the Bible, study the Bible, and understand what we are reading. It is paramount in order to live in faith. Faith comes by reading the word of God.

America was an "idea" that the settlers living in the 1750s to the 1770s started to privately talk about amongst themselves. Many of the settlers came from Europe where they felt the need to leave their homeland for various reasons, including being persecuted for their religious beliefs. Before the 1750s, the idea was to go over a great ocean to start a new life, a new beginning. The strongest military power of that day, Great Britain, ruled the land. As millions of people arrived in this new land, the British King decided to levy more and more taxes on the people. The central meeting place for most of the people was the CHURCH. The church leaders of that time listened to the people. They were in most cases not only the church leaders of their communities but also the leaders of their communities. They were bold men who recognized that they had to take a leadership role in a "revolution" to fight the King who was making life more difficult. The rest of the story as we all know is that the revolution succeeded and the United States of America was born.

We won't go into the rest of the founding of America in this book as it was spelled out in the author's last book, " Bombing America, the Deception of the American People".

This book is written to explain what the Christian American Party believes in and what it stands for. In this process, we need to examine why the existing political parties have failed the American people. Since about 1850, America has been dominated by the Democratic and Republican Parties. We will explore how these two political parties have governed us, "We the People".

No matter what your ideology is the United States of America was founded on Christian principles. That is a proven fact. If you cannot accept that you have not read the history of our founding. It was the clergy and other Christian men who dedicated their being, their fortunes, and their lives, to create a nation where they could live in freedom, in independence, where they could worship God without being persecuted. This was THE important underlying reason to create a nation where freedom and independence from a dictator king and the dictatorial Church of England, who held much power over their leaders, was the focal point of their lives. As anyone who has read our history knows, there were many miracles that God performed in order that the United States of America became a nation. Just the thought of the greatest military power in the world fighting against a rag tag bunch of colonists who for the most part had very little weapons or experience. What an amazing display of God's hand on our leaders, including George Washington who was shot three times.

As we explore today's political parties, the Democratic, Republican, and Libertarian parties, let's look if God and the Christian people are represented.

THE DEMOCRATIC PARTY

The Democratic Party is the party of social change, liberal ideas, progressive ideas, larger government, and more government in your daily lives. The Democratic Party believes the individual is incapable of taking care of himself or herself therefore they need to enact laws that provide for the individual. The Democratic Party today more reflects socialism and a socialist country idea and attitude all of which has been tried before in a number of countries and failed miserably. They believe to take from the rich and give to those who aren't is their way to even the score. The top wealthy 10% already pay close to 50% of all income taxes. The bottom 50%, those who do work but do not earn enough money to escape the so called "poverty level" along with people who don't work may receive federal subsidies. It has been widely reported through media outlets over the last 5 years that approximately 47% of Americans receive welfare payments. It has also been reported that some illegal immigrants receive some federal subsidies.

This is the Democratic Party way of governing America. Why do they want to give all the free handouts? POWER! They understand by giving Americans these free handouts these

Americans will go to the polls and vote for them, As long as a candidate has a "D" by their name these people vote for them. All these federal handouts are costing BILLIONS of dollars. But what is it doing to America? It's BANKRUPTING America.

During the past six years under Barack Obama, $8 TRILLION DOLLARS have been added to our national debt. In 2014, the revenue that came into the U.S. Treasury was $3 trillion dollars, an all time record. However, federal spending for 2014 was $3.8 trillion dollars. The more the U.S. Treasury takes in the more President Obama and the Congress spends. The U.S. national debt is now over $18 trillion dollars.

To insure even more people will vote for the Democratic Party, President Obama has had an open door policy for illegal immigrants. Many television programs have shown illegal immigrants walking across the borders as border control agents were standing by unable to enforce existing immigration laws as Obama and Attorney General Eric Holder have a policy for them to stand down. The border control agents main job has been to fill out the paperwork on anyone crossing the border. This Obama policy has caused a hardship to especially African Americans who want to find a job. No one knows the exact number of how many illegal immigrants have entered the United States in the last six years but it's estimated to be in the millions.

The talking points of both political parties when they talk about immigration on national television programs of how many illegal immigrants are in the United States has been about 12 million since about 2004. Yet, if you add the figures from the last 10 years the actual number is more like 20 million or more.

President Obama has his EPA, Environmental Protection Agency, creating havoc all over the country. From the Keystone Pipeline fiasco to trying to destroy the coal industry, to harassing farmers with water or puddle problems, to protecting some animal which isn't distinct from private industry development projects, to impossible carbon tax regulations, Obama is either shortsighted to what needs to be done or he is intentionally on an agenda.

Obama and Holder appeared not to want the integrity of the voting process to take place. They claim that the poor and minorities don't have ID cards therefore the country cannot have voter ID laws. But these poor and minorities almost all receive welfare checks which required an ID to sign up for the program. Amazingly, Obama did not win any state that required an ID, but won every state that did not require one. Think about it!

The Democratic Party supports abortion. It appears the Democratic Party is open to anyone who wants to marry each other. That opens up all kinds of possibilities. In the first month of 2015 a father has filed to marry his daughter. You may see a marriage consisting of more than two people. And sooner or later someone who believes mankind came from apes will undoubtedly marry one.

In the area of national defense Barack Obama appears to think if he declares a war to be over, it is over, even though the enemy keeps fighting.

What an imagination! Also, Obama must think by cutting our active duty military to pre- World War II levels our military gets stronger. The more he cuts, the stronger America gets. Even top generals have said America is vulnerable and could NOT SUSTAIN a war beyond a year or even fight in two areas of the world at the same time like we did in World War II. Some of you reading this may remember that Hitler had his followers who did his bidding, well Obama has his followers who do his bidding.

How do the Democrats feel about Christians? Well, the answer is that during the 2012 Democratic National Convention in North Carolina the Democratic Party delegates, these are the people who for the most part control what happens at the national and state levels, did NOT

WANT TO PUT GOD IN THEIR PLATFORM. After three voice votes of the thousands of Democratic delegates at the convention they voted against putting God in, which was witnessed on national and probably world television stations, You could hear the delegates yelling against putting God in their platform, But, there was a man of wisdom and courage who was the narrator of the voice votes, and he OVERTURNED THE DELEGATES AND DECLARED THAT GOD WILL BE IN.

Christian, do you still think the Democratic Party represents you?

Just because your family has voted a straight Democratic ticket for the last 100 years isn't it time you RE-THINK how you should vote. This isn't the same Democratic Party of 100 years ago. They have changed. Your ancestors would not recognize TODAY'S Democratic Party. Today's Democratic Party is far left. You know it's time to vote for a party that will represent you. That's the newly formed Christian American Party who will represent you.

The Democratic Party controls the most populated states with the larger cities in our country which translated in simple terms is that the people in them receive the majority of government handouts, welfare checks. How do we break this cycle? We tell them the truth! Jesus Christ died for them to offer them everlasting life if they repent their sins and live a Christian life. John 3:16 says, "God so loved the world that He gave His only begotten Son that whosoever believes in Him SHALL not perish but have everlasting life." This is the offer of SALVATION that God has given to anyone who accepts His Son and lives according to His principles. There is a judgment day. Heaven is for real. Life on this earth is only temporary, but once you get to heaven that is forever. You may live to be a 100 on earth, but you will live a thousand years in heaven. Plus you will be with our Heavenly Father and Jesus! What a wondrous time of rejoicing that will be. There is no sorrow or pain in heaven.

What am I saying. God has a plan for each of us. We only have to listen to Him. The Holy Spirit talks to us. When we are saved by accepting Jesus Christ as our Lord and Savior, the Holy Spirit comes into our life. God talks to us through the Holy Spirit. If we listen we will hear what God is saying to us. I'm just an ordinary guy. Most of us are ordinary. God has a purpose for us ordinary people. We, the ordinary people, are the ones who work and get things done. Without us the world would probably be in even more chaos. Why? Because ordinary people do exceptional things.

God gives each of us special talents. We just have to learn what our talent is and get involved. Ordinary people can do exceptional things by getting involved.

THE REPUBLICAN PARTY

While the Democratic Party will tell you what they stand for, the Republican Party, at least the last six years, will tell you they stand for anything and everything that conservatives stand for, including the Tea Party. The Republicans will campaign and promise that once elected they will solve all of our problems. Then the newly elected will go to Washington and get "schooled" by those career party politicians who have been there forever on how things really work. The awaking comes early as to who gets assignments to committees and who is ostracized. If these new do good patriots speak out too much they quickly learn the ropes and are put into line.

Speaker of the House John Boehner and Senate Majority Leader Mitch McConnell campaigned to fight tooth and nail against Obamacare, but as soon as they found their offices they fully funded Obama's health care fiasco, that's according to these two leaders, for a whole year. This has been the way it has been with these two. DECEPTION seems to be their calling card. To list what today's Republican Party actually stands for would be a waste of space because even though their platform is loaded with conservative ideas one never knows what Speaker Boehner will let them VOTE for.

The leadership in the Republican and Democratic Parties CONTROL the agendas, the legislation process, and the all important committee process which determines what gets done and how everything in Washington gets done. The U.S. Congress does not resemble a REPUBLIC, which we are, and does NOT function in a democratic way, but is tightly controlled by a very few people who are career politicians. This form is more like an oligarchy.

Each member of the U.S. House of Representatives represents approximately 700,000 people, called their constituency. Each member should have their VOICE heard and be able to represent their districts equally. But under Speaker Boehner some members are more equal than others. While under Democratic Senate Majority Leader Harry Reid the last few years the U.S. House passed over 300 bills and he wouldn't allow the Senate to discuss or vote for them.

It is often said that the United States of America is the envy of the world. Their "Democracy" is to be copied by other nations. But what happens in the United States Congress, especially the last six years is no example how a nation's government should be run.

You decide if you are happy with our present situation in Washington, where the Democrats and the Republicans keep doing the same thing no matter how many new members replace those who have been there awhile. Doing the same thing over and over again and again and expecting different results is insanity. We need a viable third party to change the culture in Washington. We need men and women who believe and stand up for Christian principles and who will stand for the founding principles of America. We need the Christian America Party.

According to one of the latest polls, 71% of Americans claim to be a Christian. The author believes by creating a new political party, the Christian American Party, Christians will finally be able to vote their beliefs, their heart, and their soul. The Christian American Party will be based on the Bible, and God's principles and values.

LIBERTARIAN PARTY

This is what you need to know about the Libertarian Party. The Libertarian Party is the party of freedom of the individual to do as he or she pleases. They make no rules or limit an individual as it relates to relationships. The Libertarian Party supports the legalization of all victimless crimes. This includes drugs, pornography, prostitution, polygamy, and homosexuality. The Libertarian Party's platform states, "government does not have the authority to define, license, or restrict personal relationships. Consenting adults should be free to choose their own sexual practices and personal relationships." This gives a group of people to be married to each other. And this would allow a man or woman to marry an animal. Remember, there are NO restrictions!

The author believes that a crime has a victim therefore how can the Libertarian Party state that there are victimless crimes.

Conclusion reference the three existing political parties, Democratic, Republican, and Libertarian, parties.

The conclusion is obvious ---- None, neither of the three parties REPRESENT CHRISTIANS OR CHRISTIAN VALUES AND PRINCIPLES.

One only has to look at the enormous mess our country is in:

1. The labor participation rate is at the lowest level it has been in since the 1970s.

2. The federal debt is over $18 trillion, ($18,000,000,000,000) dollars. Our annual total revenue is $3 trillion dollars.

3. America pays more per pupil for education than any other country in the world but according to statistics lacks in educating our students adequately.

4. Our active duty military is at pre- World War II levels. A number of GENERALS have stated that America cannot sustain a war over one year or fight in two regions of the world at the same time as we did during World War II.

5. A number of our GENERALS have stated that the world in 2015 is as dangerous as it was right before the start of World War II.

6. It appears the members of the United States Congress have become more SELF-SERVING than at any time in our history. They act more like kings and queens than like citizens. They play their little games of telling the American people one thing and not following through with

their campaign promises. Essentially nothing of real importance of solving America's problems gets done. They keep kicking the can done the road is their slogan.

7. Judges have taken God out of the public square, out of our schools, and out of our military. The politicians have stood by without combating these judges with legislation that would have stopped them.

8. Christian politicians would have found a way to stop the killing of over 50 million babies. We rarely hear of a politician in Washington go to the floor, either the Senate or House of Representatives floor, to demand a resolution of this issue.

9. These Washington politicians make laws for the American people, but EXEMPT themselves. They act -as if they are above the American people.

10. There are many other issues, but you get the point that the Democratic Party, and the Republican Party, and the Libertarian Party DO NOT REPRESENT THE AMERICAN PEOPLE.

IT IS TIME TO ELECT CHRISTIAN PEOPLE TO REPRESENT US IN WASHINGTON. WE NEED A CHRISTIAN AMERICAN PARTY. AND WE NEED IT NOW BEFORE IT GETS

TOO LATE TO TURN OUR COUNTRY BACK
ON THE RIGHT COURSE, THE COURSE OUR
FOUNDING FATHERS SET FOR US.

THE AMERICAN VOTERS

E ducation is very important! A large group of voters are uneducated about the issues. In fact a large group of American voters don't know the history of the United States of America. They don't know the Bill of Rights. They don't know the Constitution. A large group of voters depend on their political party to tell them how to vote. And a large group of American voters wait until election time to watch the political campaign ads to make up their minds on which candidate to vote for.

A large group of American voters don't know about the Christian influence in the making of America. They don't know about the miracles of the war against the most powerful nation in the world at that time, Great Britain. THEY THINK AMERICA JUST HAPPENED! They don't know that the clergy had a big hand in gathering support for the revolution. They don't know and make no effort to learn. Approximately 50% of Americans couldn't pass a basic test on American history. For years, Jay Leno of the Tonight Show would go on the streets and ask ordinary Americans basic questions about our country. Only a relatively few could answer his basic questions. And that included college graduates. The problem is that these uninformed people become voters. Many of these uninformed voters are told by a political party person to go to the voting places and given instructions on who to vote for. Is it time to require a basic history test before a person can vote?

It appears that many of our career politicians wouldn't want our voters to be more informed because it just may reduce their chances of being reelected. If we had more informed voters the politicians that "voted for a bill that you have to pass it to find out what is in it" wouldn't stand for such nonsense.

Also, a political party that controls the purse strings of America should not be able to sway the voters by giving them benefits they haven't earned. Why? Because the people who are receiving these unearned benefits will tend to vote for that political party. For example, the federal government gave out free (but the taxpayers paid for it) cell phones to millions of Americans. It appeared that most of the people who received these free cell phones called them "Obama phones". Another example, Obamacare is subsidizing approximately 75% of enrolled participants at taxpayer expense. That is how you build voters to your political party.

Statistics from the 2012 presidential election now show that Barack Obama WON ALL THE STATES THAT DO NOT REQUIRE AN ID,

BUT HE LOST ALL THE STATES THAT REQUIRE AN ID. Is this puzzling? You decide. In the author's last book, "Bombing America, the Deception of the American People" are about 40 examples that require an ID. The only reason to not require an idea are obvious. You know the answer. Even the poor who receive welfare checks need an ID to sign up for it. There have been reports that even some illegal immigrants receive welfare checks plus an ID card.

With that ID card it may be possible to vote. Some states are giving driver's licenses to illegal immigrants which includes an ID card. Also, thousands of people who have been dead for some time are still voting! If that isn't voter fraud, what is? Some people were interviewed on television admitting that they were paid to vote many times. Most of these voting problems have appeared in precincts dominated by the Democratic Party. There have been examples of over 100% people voting in certain Democratic Party controlled districts.

The odds are that if Christians were manning these precincts and districts we wouldn't continue to have these problems.

JUST HOW STUPID ARE WE? FACING THE TRUTH ABOUT THE AMERICAN VOTER — A BOOK BY RICK SHENKMAN

The book argues that although the American government has gained global political power since the late 19th century, American voters have become increasingly ignorant of politics and world affairs, and are dangerously susceptible to political manipulation. The book claims that Americans are largely incapable of critically assessing domestic and international issues, and therefore lack the knowledge and ability to participate effectively in the political process or to select political leaders in line with the national or even their own interests. Shenkman argues that voters are repeatedly and systematically misled and manipulated by politicians, and he analyzes the "dumbing down" of American politics arising from the saturation of marketing, spin machines, and misinformation in American political culture.

Shenkman offers the following facts as evidence about our electorate. Only 2 of 5 voters can name the three branches of government. And 49 percent of Americans think the president has the authority to suspend the Constitution.

The American Voter -- a book by 4 colleagues at University of Michigan "The American Voter", a book published in 1960, is a seminal study of voting behavior in the United States, authored by Angus Campbell, Philip Converse, Warren Miller, and Donald Stokes, colleagues at the University of Michigan. Among its controversial conclusions, based on one of the first comprehensive studies of election survey data (what eventually became the National Election Studies), is that most voters cast their ballots primarily on the basis of partisan identification, which is simply inherited from their parents. They also summarized that independent voters are actually the least involved in and attentive to politics. This theory of voter choice became known as the Michigan model.

Successors in the Michigan school have argued that in relying heavily on data from the 1956 presidential election, "The American Voter" drew conclusions which were not accurate over time, in particular, partisan identification has weakened since 1956.

20 REASONS AMERICA IS BECOMING AN INCREASINGLY NONFUNCTIONAL SOCIETY

John Hawkins from Townhall.com wrote an article, "20 Reasons America is Becoming an Increasingly Nonfunctional Society."

1. Starting in the sixties there was an explosion of children born out of wedlock and kids who don't grow up in two parent families fare more poorly percentage wise on just about any and every scale imaginable. The result was an explosion of substance abuse, teenage pregnancies, suicide rates, and homelessness. The mother was the single family member.

2. Many people are becoming so childlike in their dependence on the government that they can't save for their own retirement, escape from an oncoming hurricane, or even purchase their own birth control without the government handling it for them.

3. Our legal system encourages frivolous lawsuits, is punitively expensive, and because of the political inclinations of the judges, can often be almost random.

4. Leeching off more productive people has become much more acceptable. To many people,

taking welfare, food stamps, free lunches, and anything else they can get the government to force someone else to pay isn't shameful; it's deserved, presumably because they're doing everyone else in the country such a wonderful favor just by existing.

5. The mainstream media has become so partisan for the Democratic Party that it's not significantly different from a state run media. Every news story and scandal is reported differently based solely on which party is involved. "Scandals" that would destroy the careers of Republicans are largely ignored and treated as irrelevant when Democrats are involved.

6. Americans have lost confidence in our institutions. Most Americans don't trust our politicians, our criminal justice system, big business, our schools, our media, or our churches.

7. As choices have proliferated because of the Internet, TV, and our affluent culture, Americans have become more alien to each other and share less and less cultural experiences.

8. Our movies, music, and TV shows are provided by people who are almost universally hostile to conservatism, Christianity and traditional American values.

9. We have stopped breaking up monopolies in this country and that has allowed mega-corporations to have an outsized and unhealthy level of influence on our political process. That's how corporations that make more money every sixty seconds than the average person does in a lifetime can rake in hundreds of millions each year in subsidies and be given access to billions of dollars' worth of your money when they make dumb decisions that put their companies' future at risk.

10. Our country was founded on Judeo-Christian values and yet Christianity in this country is slowly retreating from Biblical principles, the Public Square, and American life in general.

11. Women becoming educated, moving into the work force and becoming much more independent has been a positive development. However, the downside of it is that it has led to later marriages, a soaring divorce rate, more out of wedlock birth, and much more conflict, discontent, and fights over children between the sexes. Marriage and relationships are an order of magnitude more complicated for Americans today than they were sixty years ago.

12. Gerrymandering, increasing partisanship, and a lack of term limits have allowed politics to become a lifetime job for a majority of members of Congress. The average congressman cannot be

defeated by a member of the opposing party and only has to worry about making special interest groups on his side angry enough to back a primary challenger against him. For most members of Congress, once they're elected once, they never have to worry about voters in their own district.

13. The differences between the Republican and Democratic Party have become so great that there is very little common ground anymore. Not only do both parties propose very different solutions to America's problems, but both sides also see the other side's solutions as taking the country in exactly the wrong direction.

14. Over the past few decades both parties, but particularly the Democrats, have given up on the idea that government should have any sort of limits on what it spends, should be required to afford new spending, or should even try to pay back the money it already owes.

15. Schools have moved away from teaching reading, writing, history, morality, and patriotism for the benefit of the students to pushing self-esteem and liberal indoctrination for the benefit of the teachers' unions and salaries of professors.

16. Our entire society is based on a Constitution that is being systematically ignored, distorted, and

treated as optional by the populace, our politicians, and even the judges who are sworn to enforce it.

17. Our federal government has grown so far beyond the boundaries that were originally intended for it by the Founding Fathers that it intrudes and interferes into almost every facet of American life. Since the government is always slower, stupider, and less efficient than the private sector it feeds off to grow, this leads to an inevitable decline.

18. The Democratic Party's entire strategy is based around giving people money and goods that they didn't earn and ginning up hatred between different groups of Americans.

19. As the standard of living in America has increased and globalism has made having manual labor done in foreign countries more economical, highly paid, low skill level jobs have mostly either have been replaced by technology or have moved offshore to nations with cheaper labor. This means that a large number of men who could have once held "good" jobs that could have provided a living for them and a family now are barely able to take care of themselves and they also have poor future prospects in an economy that now favors highly educated, heavily skilled workers.

20. Race and ideology based tribalism is becoming the norm. Different racial and political groups often have completely different standards, moral codes, and types of behavior depending on whether the person they're dealing with is a member of their own "tribe".

ONE CONGRESSIONAL ACHIEVEMENT: LEGALIZING WHAT USED TO BE VIEWED AS CORRUPTION — BY ALLAN C. BROWNFIELD OF THE FITZGERALD GRIFFIN FOUNDATION

Congress, for good reason, is held in disrepute by most Americans. The latest Gallup Poll tells us that only eight percent of Americans think Congress is doing a good job. It is difficult to imagine who these eight percent might be, other than relatives or employees of those holding office.

But if Congress has no inclination to fulfill its constitutional responsibilities when it comes to going to war, or balancing the budget, protecting our borders, or performing the many other essential tasks left undone, it has been successful in one area. Both Republicans and Democrats, in bipartisan cooperation, have done their best to legalize their own conduct, which in many cases, used to be viewed as corruption.

In an important new book, "Corruption in America: From Benjamin Franklin's Snuff Box to Citizens United", Professor Zephyr Teachout of Fordham Law School argues that corruption is the most pressing problem our democracy faces. In her view, corruption — broadly understood as placing private interests over the public good in public office — is at the root of what ails American government.

The Framers themselves predicted that corruption would be a constant threat. George Mason warned, "if we do not provide against corruption, our government will soon be at an end". In James Madison's notebook from the summer of 1787, "corruption" appears 54 times.

Teachout writes, "Corruption, influence, and bribery were discussed more often in the convention than factions, violence, or instability."

By corruption, the Founders did not mean simply the exchange of cash for votes, what the Supreme Court in Citizens United came to call "quid pro quo corruption." Teachout reports that the word "corruption" came up hundreds of times in the Constitutional Convention and the ratification debates, yet "only a handful of uses referred to what we might now think of as quid pro quo bribes," constituting "less than one-half of one percent of the times corruption was raised."

The Framers believed that corruption involved using public office for private ends, which was the opposite of public virtue. A republican form of government required that men act as citizens concerned for the public good, not as private, self-interested individuals.

The philosopher Baron de Montesquieu, who had great influence on the founding Fathers, maintained," the misfortune of a republic happens when the people are gained by bribery and corruption: in this case, they grow indifferent to public affairs, and avarice becomes their predominant passion."

James Madison believed that without civic virtue, "no theoretical checks, no form of government, can render us secure. To suppose that any form of government will secure liberty or happiness without any virtue in the people is a chimerical idea."

Professor David Cole of the Georgetown Law School notes, "The concern with corruption, broadly conceived, has remained a dominant theme of American law and politics. Indeed, because of these concerns, lobbying itself was treated as illegal for much of the nation's history."

"This seems inconceivable in today's political culture, in which "K Street" lobbying dominates Washington's political and financial economies alike. But until the twentieth century, lobbying was considered contrary to public policy. Some states such as Georgia made it a crime.

And even where lobbying was not a crime, courts refused to enforce contracts for lobbying on the ground that such conduct was contrary to public policy."

Consider the 1874 case of "Trist vs. Child", in which the Supreme Court declined to enforce a contract for lobbying. N.P. Trist, an elderly man to frail to travel to Washington, hired a lawyer, Linus Child, to try to persuade Congress to authorize the payment of an 18 year old debt owed to Trist. Trist told Child he would get one-fourth of the recovery as his fee, When Child succeeded, however, Trist's son refused payment, and Child sued to recover the fee.

The Supreme court declined to enforce the contract. Lobbying was contrary to public policy because the lobbyist was paid to advocate not for the public good, but for someone's private interest. It risked corrupting the political process. The Court reasoned that if individuals were allowed to hire lobbyists, soon corporations would be doing so, a practice "every right minded man would instinctively denounce."

The Court declared: "If any of the great corporations of the country were to hire adventurers who make market of themselves in this way, to procure the passage of a general law with a view to the promotion of their private interests, the moral sense of every right minded man would instinctively denounce the employer and employed as steeped in corruption, and the employment as infamous."

In 1974, only 3% of retiring or defeated members of Congress became lobbyists. Today, that number is 42% for members of the House and 50% for Senators. In 2010, Senator Evan Bayh (D-IN), after writing in The New York Times about the "corrosive system of campaign financing," joined with Andrew Card, the former Bush chief of staff, in the U.S. Chamber of Commerce to lobby against corporate regulatory reform. After its oil spill in the Gulf, BP recruited a former top spokesman for Dick Cheney and the Democratic fundraiser Tony Podesta as lobbyists.

Two of the three political action committee donors to former Democratic Senate Majority Leader Harry Reid and Republican Senate Majority leader Mitch McConnell are the same: Comcast and AT&T, Former Republican Senate Leader Trent Lott and former Democratic House Leader Dick Gephardt are united in lobbying for GE. And members of Congress often go to work, for million dollar salaries, for the very industries they were responsible for regulating while in Congress. Former House Majority Leader Eric Cantor, who regulated banking in Congress, is now at work on Wall Street. And this clear conflict of interest is legal, because members of Congress, in bipartisan agreement, have made it so.

Trust in our government is eroding. In 1964, 29% of voters believed that government was "run by a few big interests looking out for themselves." By 2013, 79% felt that way. In 2006, 59% of Americans were convinced that corruption in government was widespread: by 2013, that number had jumped to 79%.

Since Congress writes the laws, we have seen members of both parties make legal what would ordinarily be viewed as corruption. Consider Leadership PACs, which permit politicians to solicit and spend money without the same restrictions they face when using their campaign committees.

According to Peter Schweitzer, a fellow at the Hoover Institution of Stanford University, these groups have become slush funds that enable lavish lifestyles while they exist, in theory, to help members of Congress finance their own campaigns and help political allies. He cites such examples as these:

1, Senator Saxby Chambliss (R-GA) presided over a leadership PAC that spent $10,000 on golf at Pebble Beach; nearly $27,000 at Ruth's

Chris Steakhouse; and $107,752 at the Breakers resort in Palm Beach, Florida.

2. Senator Roy Blount (R--MO) spent $65,000 at a resort at Kiawah Island, South Carolina.

3. Rep. Charles Rangel (D-NY) used his leadership PAC to spend $64,500 on a painting of himself.

4. Rep. Rosa DeLauro (D-CT) used hers to pay for catered parties at her home several times a month.

Beyond the abuse of money, Members of Congress regularly pass laws for the rest of us from which they exempt themselves. In the recent controversy over the Affordable Care Act, Americans learned that Congressional staff members were to receive subsidies not available to other Americans.

Traditionally, Congress has exempted itself from laws and regulations it imposes upon other Americans ---- from Social Security, to affirmative action, to occupational health and safety rules. Recently, Senator Rand Paul (R-KY) introduced a Constitutional amendment stating, "Congress shall make no law applicable to a citizen of the United States that is not equally applicable to congress." (Many conservatives have asked for this to be the 28th Amendment for years.)

Much time is spent lamenting the "gridlock" in Congress. But there is bipartisan cooperation between Republicans and Democrats, liberal and conservatives, when it comes to making legal what has historically viewed as corruption, and which most Americans properly understand to be corruption today. The fears of the Founding Fathers have become our current reality, to the detriment of all ---- except the favored few who have enriched themselves at the public trough and cleverly avoid any penalty for doing so by making their self-serving acts perfectly legal.

FRANKLIN GRAHAM: CHRISTIANS MUST SPEAK OUT, GET POLITICAL

R ev. Franklin Graham has urged Christians "to get involved in government" and "in politics" and speak out about the future of the country even if their political opponents will attack them for doing so., CNS News reported.

In a speech in Oklahoma, Graham said that because "gays and lesbians are in politics" along "with the anti-God people," Christians have no choice but to enter the political fray.

"I'm here to tell you, church, God loves each and every one and Christ died for our sins, and we've got a responsibility to take this message to the ends of the earth," Graham said in the January 26th speech to the Oklahoma State Evangelism Conference, 'and I want to encourage you to take a stand in your communities."

Graham -- head of the Billy Graham Evangelistic Association founded by his father -- said Christians needed to follow God.

Graham said, "the only hope is that this country repents of its sins and turns once again to the God of our fathers. "

GEORGE WASHINGTON'S EXAMPLE
ON RELIGIOUS LIBERTY

Article from the Morning Bell of The Heritage Foundation. George Washington was not simply a President. He was the "indispensible man of the American Founding. Washington's words, thoughts, and deeds as a military commander, a President, and a patriotic leader make him arguably the greatest statesman in our history.

All Presidents can learn from Washington's leadership in foreign policy, in upholding the rule of law, and -- especially now -- in the importance of religion and religious liberty. While the Obama Administration claims to be "accommodating" Americans' religious freedom concerns regarding the Health and Human Services (HHS) Obamacare mandate, it is actually trampling religious freedom. President Washington set a tremendous example for the way that Presidents should handle such conflicts.

Washington knew that religion and morality are essential to creating the conditions for decent politics. "Where" Washington asked, "is the security for property, for reputation, for life, if the sense of religious obligation desert the oaths which are the instruments of investigation in courts of justice?"

"Religion and morality are," Washington wrote, "essential to the happiness of mankind: A volume could not trace all their connections with private and public felicity."

To match his high praise of religion, Washington had a robust understanding of religious liberty. Freedom allows religion, in the form of morality and through the teachings of religion, to exercise an unprecedented influence over private and public opinion. Religious liberty shapes mores, cultivates virtues, and provides an independent source of moral reasoning and authority. In his letter to the Newport Hebrew congregation -- at the time the largest community of Jewish families in America -- President Washington grounded America's religious and civil liberties in natural rights, and not mere toleration.

Washington also confronted the limits of religious liberty. In one letter, Washington praised the Quakers for being good citizens but chastised their pacifism. "Your principles and conduct are well known to me; and it is doing the people called Quakers no more than justice to say, that (except their declining to share with others the burden of the common defense) there is no denomination among us, who are more exemplary and useful citizens." Yet Washington ended his letter assuring them of his "wish and desire that the laws always be as extensively accommodated to their practice."

Such a true accommodation upholds the rule of law and religious liberty, because it allows men and women of religious faith to follow the law and their faith.

In his letter to the Quakers, Washington explained that government is instituted to "protect the persons and consciences of men from oppression.

Further, it was the duty of rulers not only to abstain from oppression themselves, but, according to their stations, to prevent it in others."

Washington's advice has gone unheeded.

Today, in fact since the 1940s, we are told that religion and politics require a strict separation; that religion is a hindrance to happiness and therefore has been gradually stripped from the public square. We're told that displays of religious faith don't support the community but are downright offensive to non-adherents. The Supreme Court has supported and extenuated this tortured logic. Since the 1940s, the Court has put religion and religious liberty into a smaller box. At best, religion is a private good. but one that should not be presented to others.

And religious beliefs have no bearing on public life.

We can see where this logic goes. Under Obamacare all insurance plans must cover, at no cost to the insured, abortion inducing drugs, contraceptives, sterilization, and patient education and counseling for women of reproductive age. Illustrating the Obama Administration's narrow view of religion, only formal houses of worship are afforded an exemption from the coercive mandate. Many other religious employers such as Catholic hospitals, Christian schools, and faith based pregnancy care centers are forced to provide and pay for coverage of services that, as a matter of faith, they find morally objectionable.

George Washington was the directing spirit without which there would be no independence, no country (no United States of America), and no Constitution.

E very American has heard of the ACLU. The ACLU is a group that is working to destroy America's Judeo-Christian heritage. Some of their successes include:

1. Removing nativity scenes from public property.

2. Banning songs such as Silent Night from schools.

3. Refusing to allow students to write about the Christian aspect of Christmas in school projects.

4. Renaming Christmas break Winter break.

5. Refusing to allow a city sponsored Christmas parade to be called a Christmas parade.

6. Not allowing a Christmas tree in a public school.

7. Sue states to force them to legalize homosexual marriage.

8. Force libraries to remove porn filters from their computers.

9. Sue the Boy Scouts to force them to accept homosexuals as scout leaders.

10. Censor student led prayer at graduation.

11. Trying to remove "under God" from the Pledge of Allegiance.

12. Trying to remove "In God We Trust" from our currency.

RONALD REAGAN

In his inaugural speech on January 20, 1981, Reagan announced that " government is not the solution to our problems; government is the problem."

He called for an era of national renewal and hoped that America would again be a "beacon of hope for those who do not have freedom." The 1970s was a tough time in America with the Nixon problems and the failed Carter administration. America needed hope and inspiration.

On March 31, 1981, only a few months after becoming President, Reagan was exiting the Washington Hilton hotel with several of his advisors, shots rang out and quick thinking Secret Service agents thrust Reagan into his limousine. Once in the car, aides discovered that Reagan had been hit. At the hospital, doctors determined that the gunman's bullet had pierced one of the President's lungs and narrowly missed his heart.

Within several weeks after the shooting, Reagan was back to work. God's hand was on Ronald Reagan and the United States of America. Ronald Reagan became one of America's greatest Presidents. An amazing story of American history as two of our greatest Presidents, George Washington and Ronald Reagan, both were shot.

God is in control of all things and has worked His miracles to protect America. (Only now during the last 6 years as our President Obama has declared America is NOT a Christian nation are we in real trouble. If you know your history of the world it has been when a leader of a nation has denied the Christian God and proclaimed that to the world, that nation has been defeated).

On the domestic front, President Reagan advanced policies that reduced social programs and restrictions on business. Tax cuts were implemented to stimulate the United States' economy. He also advocated for increase in military (primarily because President Jimmy Carter had decimated the American military). By 1983, the nation's economy had begun to recover and, according to many economists, entered a seven year period of prosperity. In foreign affairs, Reagan led the defeat of the Soviet Union.

In November 1984, Ronald Reagan was re-elected in a landslide. Reagan carried 49 of the 50 U.S. states in the election, and received 525 of 538 electoral votes -- the largest number ever won by an American presidential candidate.

MARGARET THATCHER

Margaret Thatcher was the leader of the United Kingdom, more commonly called Great Britain for over 11 years, from 1979 to 1991. Thatcher was a strong conservative woman who believed in freedom, liberty, democracy, quality of life, and individual responsibility. In a statement published in a magazine, Margaret Thatcher is quoted:

I think we have gone through a period when too many children and people have been given to understand, "I have a problem, it is the Government's job to cope with it", or "I have a problem, I will go and get a grant to cope with it!" " I am homeless, the Government must house me!" And so they cast their problems on society and who is society? There is no such thing! There are individual men and women and there are families and no government can do anything except through people and people look to themselves first. It is our duty to look after ourselves and then also to help look after our neighbour and life is a reciprocal business and people have got the entitlements too much in mind without the obligations."

Margaret Thatcher worked closely with President Reagan, and together they helped shape a decade of positive conservative advances.

Their contributions were important in getting the world through a difficult time during the Cold War with the Soviet Union.

REVEREND BILLY GRAHAM

Most people know that Rev. Billy Graham preached all over the world and his ministry has brought millions of people worldwide to accept Jesus Christ as Lord and Savior of their life. But it is not universally known how Billy Graham helped Rev. Martin Luther King, Jr.

In 1957, Graham stance on integration became more publicly shown when he allowed African American ministers Thomas Kilgore and Gardner Taylor to serve as members of his New York Crusade's executive committee, and invited the Rev. Martin Luther king, Jr., whom he first met during the Montgomery Bus Boycott in 1955, to join him in the pulpit at his 16 week revival in New York City, where 2.3 million gathered at Madison Square Garden, Yankee Stadium, and Times Square to hear them. Rev. Billy Graham and Rev. Martin Luther King, Jr. became good friends.

In 1963, Graham posted bail for King to be released from jail during the civil rights protests in Birmingham, Alabama. Graham held integrated crusades in Birmingham, Alabama, on Easter 1964 in the aftermath of the bombing of the Sixteenth Street Baptist Church, and toured Alabama again in the wake of the violence that accompanied the first Selma to Montgomery march in 1965.

Rev. Billy Graham has been at the forefront of doing God's work in America and around the world.

EDUCATION

Education is the right of every American citizen. That has been assumed to mean a FREE education from the first grade through the twelve grade.

There are families that choose not to use the public schools. These are mainly the Catholics who use Catholic schools, the rich who send their children to expensive private schools, and some people who home school their children. The education in these schools has proven to be comparable to the public schools. In some cases even proven to be better. And at a cost per pupil far less than the public schools. (the author has no idea what the cost per pupil is in the expensive private schools).

It appears that cost per pupil has become much more important to the public schools than the actual education of the students. Many, if not most public schools, have more non-teaching employees on their payroll than they have teachers. They are all counted as part of the education process. The cost of the administrators, the special counselors, the lawyers, the union reps, and the teachers has gone through the roof.

Their salaries, health care, and retirement benefits has created a major problem for those who have to pay them, the American taxpayer. In the state of Kansas the cost of education consumes over half of the state budget. And these so called educators are suing for even more. There must be a point where the education of the students is MEASURED by how much they are learning instead of how much the taxpayers have to pay per student. If you continue to throw money at a problem and the results don't measure up then a new course should be taken. Albert Einstein said, "if you keep doing the same thing over and over again, you can't expect different results." Most people admit Einstein is right. And by most accounts he was an intelligent man.

This author spent 20 years in the public school system. The first 12 years, then 4 years for his Bachelor's Degree, then 2 year for the Master's Degree, and then 2 years working on his PhD. This author attended 8 schools the first 12 years of school, including going to 3 high schools in 4 years. (Dad was in the military for 20 years). That's experiencing a whole lot of teachers. He can count on one hand the truly outstanding teachers that he had. Most of the teachers were good. There were some that were really bad. All we expect is that the teacher is good. This author worked in two universities for four years. There is a lot of waste in education and low standards. In the author's opinion, the quality of teachers at the university level are even lower than the high school level which is lower than the elementary level.

How do we get teachers that know the subject they are teaching, and teachers that also know how to teach? Should we require teachers to gain at least 5 years of experience in the real world, in the private sector, before they are eligible to teach? It's no wonder the American public school system is now considered second rate among the western world education systems. And we are spending far more than any country in the world for education.

According to an article by Dan Mitchell of the Cato Institute, the United States spent $15,171 on each student ---- more than any other nation.

Switzerland was second in spending per pupil at $14,922. The average spending per pupil was $9,313.

The United States routinely trails its rival countries in performances on international exams. U.S. fourth graders are 11th in the world in math in the Trends in International Mathematics and Science Study. U.S. eighth graders ranked ninth in math, according to the 2011 results.

The Program for International Student Assessment found the United States ranked 31st in math literacy among 15 year old students and below the international average. The same 2009 tests found the United States ranked 23rd in science. The average high school teacher in the United States earns about $53,000 per year well above the international average. And that isn't counting for the health care and retirement benefits the American teacher receives.

Dan Mitchell's summary is that the United States has a very costly and inefficient government, public school, monopoly.

Some statistics prove that ever since the U.S. Department of Education was created that education started going downhill. It appears that the more money the Department of Education gets and spends the lower the student performance has become. It may be due in part that every new Secretary of Education has his or her agenda on what our education system should look like. From new math, to no child left behind, to every child should have their own computer in school, to not teaching the basics of reading, writing, and arithmetic, to common core, just to mention a few of the latest trends. No wonder we are failing our students. If we don't know by now what works and what doesn't, then we are throwing good money away.

There is a push by many people that want the LOCAL School Board of Education to determine what is being taught in their public schools. Boy, that sounds great! But once you look in the lack of standards of who can be elected to the LOCAL School Board then you realize that is not the answer. LOCAL School Board members are elected by their local communities, but THERE ARE NO QUALIFICATIONS TO BE ELECTED TO THIS BOARD. THIS BOARD COULD CONSIST OF HIGH SCHOOL DROPOUTS. Do you want high school dropouts to have this authority and responsibility?

In the author's opinion, the solution is to have each state determine the standards for their public schools. EACH STATE SHALL CREATE STANDARDS FOR THEIR PUBLIC SCHOOL SYSTEMS, INCLUDING GRADES 1-THROUGH 12, AND THE UNIVERSITIES IN THEIR STATES. The qualifications of each state Department of Education employee shall be:

1. 50% of their staff employees will have a minimum of 20 years experience in the private sector.

2. no more than 20% of their staff employees shall be lawyers.

3. 20% of their staff employees shall have a minimum of 10 years of teaching experience.

4. 10% of their staff employees shall be experienced researchers.

5. Every employee shall have a college degree. It is suggested that they have an advanced degree.

It is recommended that the United States Congress SHALL reduce the spending for the United States Department of Education by 25% each year for a period of 3 years. The remaining 25% of employees will work with each state Department of Education coordinating the information learned of educational processes that actually work in furthering our nation's public school systems to achieve excellence.

MONEY

One can write a book about money, and many people have. But, for this effort to present the views of a new political party, the Christian American Party, will concentrate on other issues. The author realizes that very little is ever done without having enough money. And most of the issues presented require money as money is the driving force in today's politics.

In the 1930's, paper money was redeemable for precious metals that were set at a fixed price, $35 for an ounce of gold. In 1971, President Richard Nixon ended the trading of gold at this fixed price. Now, paper money is a medium of exchange, otherwise worthless in material value.

The amount of paper money circulating in the nation is no longer restricted by the amount of gold/silver in Fort Knox but a return to the gold standard is not practical. The federal budget alone approaches $4 trillion dollars (Obama proposal for FY 2015) and at $1000 per ounce, this alone would amount to an unwieldy 4 billion ounces of gold.

FEDERAL RESERVE

We won't go into the history or try to explain all the Federal Reserve system is involved with. Here are just a few questions:

1. Is the Federal Reserve constitutional?

2. Is the Federal Reserve controlled by wealthy bankers?

3. Does the Federal Reserve charge interest from the money it prints and loans to the United States government?

4. What is backing the money the Federal Reserve prints and loans to our government?

5. Why is there no transparency for what the Federal Reserve does?

6. Why has there not been an audit or investigation how the Federal Reserve operates?

TAXES

The Christian American Party advocates an overhaul of the tax code as well as a reduction of taxes.

The federal government derives revenues from a myriad of taxes on the American people and corporations. The federal tax code is quite long and complex. Legislators seem not to know just how long the tax code is. (trygve.com/taxcode) states, "So, depending on whom you ask, our elected representatives are of the opinion that this particular section of the United States code is somewhere between 2,500 and 2,500,000 pages long."

But (townhall.com/columnists/politicalcalculations) states, "According to the CCH Standard Federal Tax Reporter, as of 2013, it now takes 73,954 regular 81/2 by 11 sheets of paper to explain the complexity of the U.S. federal tax code!" Considering 2 pages per sheet, it is 147,908 pages long.

President Ronald Reagan said that there are more than 151 taxes on a loaf of bread. And the chicken didn't put the 100 taxes on an egg.

Legislators are becoming hard pressed to find and create more tax sources, but liberal spenders are creative in taxing and spending; the end is not in sight.

There are too many tax loopholes. Some examples are:

1. The rich have a capital gains tax advantage, estimated by the Joint Committee on Taxation to cost the U.S. Treasury nearly $457 billion dollars between 2011 and 2015. The rich are able to pay lower tax rates.

2. U.S. Multinational corporations don't pay taxes to the U.S. on overseas profits until and if they transfer them into the U.S.

3. There are deductions for U.S. corporations for shipping jobs overseas. This includes incentives for offshore production.

4. There is a loop hole using an accounting procedure whereby corporations may purchase something say for $30 earlier in the year and more at $45 later and when selling them at $50 they would only pay taxes on $5 profit.

5. Accelerated appreciation deduction allows corporations to deduct depreciation of equipment at a faster rate than it actually depreciates.

Corporate taxes increase the cost of production. These increases in costs are passed on to the consumers of the product as long as the competition from the manufacturers permits. Sometimes a manufacturer may be forced into offshore production in order to avoid taxes and remain competitive. Corporate taxes, being passed on to consumers, can be considered consumer taxes.

There are also tax loop holes for individuals, but we won't go into these as we hopefully have made the point that our tax code needs to be reformed.

SPENDING

The Christian American Party advocates less government spending and a balanced budget.

What should be of great concern to the American taxpayer are the budget items called "pork". These are unwarranted handouts intended to placate a politician's constituency, this includes government waste and payback to donors of large campaign contributions. Legislators will earmark funds for pet projects to keep their constituents happy. In the annual appropriations bills containing 1,924 pages, Senator John McCain identified 6,488 earmarks totaling nearly $8.3 billion dollars. (www. businessinsider.com).

There are numerous federal government "freebies" available to most Americans. It has created an increase in government control and government itself. It has also created a great harm as an increasing number of Americans are unable or unwilling to shift for themselves. They have become the dependent class. And they are demanding ever more freebies. The number of those receiving freebies almost equals the number of people who are paying for them.

There are just too many problems associated with the reckless spending of Washington politicians to address in this book.

INTERNATIONAL FAIR TRADE POLICIES

F oreign trade policies must more aggressively reflect the concept of fair trade as a matter of retaining jobs in America. According to Wikipedia, both NAFTA (North Atlantic Free Trade Association) and CAFTA (Central American Free Trade Association) facilitated off shoring and hence contributed to loss of American jobs. Many American corporations locate off shore mainly to use lower cost foreign labor and to escape excessive taxation and over regulation.

A factor affecting loss of American jobs is the unfair trading practices of a country that devalues its currency deliberately. The government fixes the relative price of its currency below the present level and prohibits currency exchanges at any other rate. If country "A" undervalues its currency, the goods from foreign countries in country "A" become over priced and simultaneously country "A's" goods in other countries are at bargain prices.

LOBBYING

Corporations, associations, special interest groups and even individuals attempt to influence government officials and legislators to gain benefits of one kind or another. Political action committees obtain contributions from members to campaign for candidates for political office or to influence legislation. Their clout is a voter block, funds for office seeking candidates and even funding lavish parties.

Although lobbying is considered to be a form of free speech, there are rules lobbyists must abide by, but the Supreme Court allowed big corporations ---- including foreign corporations ---- to spend unlimited amounts of money to influence our elections. Most people would agree that this is harmful to the election process and to governance, seemingly bringing governance for sale to the highest bidder. There has been little reform since that Supreme Court decision. It seems that present methods of financing campaigns contribute significantly to a government that is not solely by and for the people but somewhat by and for large donors and for their interests. Reform is needed.

The enormous amount of money it takes to finance a candidate's run for political office is available from lobbyists is tempting even though the candidate's impartiality may become compromised. Federal Election Commission rules allow former law makers to give their unused funds to charities, political parties, or candidates, or to pay campaign debt, but do not allow personal use. An article by Al Kamen and Colby Itkowitz in the Washington Post of May 22, 2014, stated, " Dozens of former members of Congress and failed candidates are collectively hoarding close to $100 million dollars in their dusty campaign coffers." Some may be holding these for funds for future campaigns, but charities could make good use of the rest.

The author believes that we need to completely reform the whole idea of lobbying and lobbyists. We need to return to what the Founding Fathers intended as it relates to this issue. Why should wealthy people and organizations be allowed to lobby and the average American doesn't have the financial means to be represented? Wasn't America founded for the people and by the people instead of for the wealthy to dominate and control the proceedings of government?

If you, the reader of this book, will help this author to form and establish the Christian American Party, together we can reform not only this lobbying crisis we now have but the whole political situation we have in the Congress of the

United States of America. We want our legislators to have integrity and represent "WE THE PEOPLE" as it was originally designed by our Founding Fathers.

If a person is elected to the United States Congress for even only 2 years they receive a retirement pension at their salary of $174,00 dollars a year for life. Compare that to a person who serves 20 years in the military who risks his or her life and receives a fraction of what a Congress person receives. We need to reform this system where our elected officials are treated more like average citizens than like kings and queens.

MARRIAGE

God made man and woman. He made them to naturally be together. He made them to be fruitful and to populate the earth. He gave them feelings for each other, called love. He made man to be masculine. He made woman to be feminine. the concept of marriage between a man and a woman is according to the Word of God. This is an interesting fact that appeared to work for thousands of years. If you know the history of mankind through the centuries you know this to be true. The Bible states the genealogy of the human race through the man and specifically the advancement of Christianity. The genealogy is from Adam to Abraham to Moses to David to Jesus and all those in between, generation after generation. The Christian line OF succession ALL came from the SAME family.

Over the centuries, especially the last two, the woman has become equal to the man in the western civilized world. This phenomena is the result of the man not having led his family and nation according to God's purposes and principles. God had a plan of how life and events would progress from generations to generations EVEN BEFORE HE CREATED THE WORLD. He knew that man would have shortcomings therefore He elevated the woman to be his partner.

God made the woman to be more compassionate and that trait was needed to revolutionize the world from the continuous man made world of wars. Civilization in the modern era of the world has become more compassionate in large part to the advancement of religion and education which occurred in the family households and by the elevation of the woman.

Since 1945, the wars that have been fought have mainly begun in the areas of the world where at the time of conflict those nations were not as advanced as the westernized nations. But the western nations got involved in order to quell the conflict and try to restore peace. Examples of this is Korea, Vietnam, and the Middle East. The Europeans have finally had peace among themselves for the first time in history.

God made man and woman. He told them to multiply. That infers they can have sex, but was intended to be in a marriage relationship. Having a baby outside of marriage is considered a sin. Everyone who is honest with themselves knows that once the woman becomes pregnant that woman is having a baby. The question should NOT be at what age can the baby be killed. If the woman for whatever reason does not want the baby or cannot take care of the baby she should give birth and then inform the proper authorities to that fact. There are many families that will love that baby as if he or she is their own. The adoption process should be quick and as painless as possible. There have been countless examples of women who wanted to abort their baby but at the last minute changed their mind and these babies grew up in a loving home and contributed to the advancement of our society. There have been over 50 million babies killed since Roe vs. Wade became law in the United States. That's a sin of the courts, the politicians, and everyone who supports this law. They will answer to God on judgment day. God may ask the lawyers of our country why didn't you stop this or why didn't you bring a case to the courts to stop this. God may ask every politician who has served in the Congress of the United States of America what legislation did you sponsor to stop this. Jesus said that if you deny ME before man, I will deny you before My Father in Heaven. There will be NO excuses. A politician's first responsibility is to God.

HELPFUL IDEAS TO LIVING A CHRISTIAN LIFE

The following ideas are intended to help, to encourage, to enjoy, and to hopefully be an inspiration to do your best. One idea per page is in the hope that you will think and reflect on each idea.

Take CONTROL of your life.

You learn from everything you do.

Create your OWN BOOK on life. Write things down. Important things. Read it over and over

Define yourself. Who are you? What do you really want out of life?

YOU alone can answer ---- Do you want to be a BIG FISH in a LITTLE pond ---- or do you want to be a LITTLE fish in a BIG ocean?

Ask yourself ---- What is real?   What is good?

No man is justified in doing evil on the ground of expedience.
By Theodore Roosevelt

Change is the ONLY constant that exists.

ORDER ---- A place for everything, ----
everything in its place.
by Benjamin Franklin

Don't resist change ---- you may be left behind.

Exercise your body and your mind.

Time is precious ---- Don't waste it!

Be a professional in the true sense of the word. In everything you do, do it in a professional manner.

Appreciate value ---- and give value.

Do everything with CLASS

Learn to live in the present moment

Become more patient

Let others have the glory

Never underestimate the power of a kind
word or deed

Experience is not what happens to a
man.
It is what a man does with what happens to
him.
Aldous Huxley

Don't use time or words carelessly ----
neither can be retrieved

Look for opportunities to make people feel important

Thinking is the hardest work there is, which is probably the reason so few engage in it.
By Henry Ford

Leave everything a little better than you found it.

There is no way to know before
experiencing it

After all is said and done, much is said and little is done.

Make peace with imperfection

Most of our lives are about proving something, either to ourselves or to someone else.

Practice humility

Character is that which reveals moral purpose, exposing the class of things a man chooses or avoids
By Aristotle

In life every great enterprise begins with and takes its first step in faith
By Schlegel

Success may come tomorrow ---- if you quit
today you may never know

The difference between success and failure
may be a very thin line

Money is a good servant, but a poor master
By Dominque Bouheurs

Never take anything for granted

Humor is the best medicine. Learn to laugh. Learn to have fun.

The highest use of capital is not to make money, but to make money do more for the betterment of life.
Henry Ford

Learn to be a good listener

Life is a journey

See problems as opportunities for growth

Most people are willing to pay more to be
amused than to be educated
By Robert C. Savage

Inspiration ---- Ronald Reagan was a senior citizen before he was President

Money is NOT the root of all evil. What's important is how you make your money and what you do with it.

Don't take advantage of people to get ahead

There is right and wrong. Sometimes the consequences of our actions taken turn out wrong. It is important to do what is right, we cannot control the results as we cannot control other people.

Be a good loser.   Be a good winner.

Pay attention to the details

Schedule TIME for what is important

You can't escape the responsibility of tomorrow by evading it today.
By Abraham Lincoln

Others can stop you temporarily, only you
can do it permanently

Beware of the person who has nothing to
lose

Never compromise your integrity. Never!

The gem cannot be polished without friction, nor man perfected without trials.
Chinese Proverb

Don't be stubborn

Don't be afraid to say, "I don't know"

Anger and intolerance are the twin enemies
of correct understanding
By   Gandhi

When anger rises, think of the consequences
By Confucius

Accept the fact that life isn't fair

Criticize the performance, not the performer

If you don't start, it's certain you won't finish

FREEDOM ----- NEVER TAKE
FREEDOM FOR GRANTED. NEVER

Honor those who have served in the military. They may have risked their life for you and our country

Read the Constitution of the United States of
America ---- every year

Whatever you are trying to avoid won't go away until you confront it

One thing we have learned from history is that history repeats itself

BE A SELF STARTER

Don't let anyone or anything become so important that it consumes you

Spend your money wisely ----- invest in yourself

Learn to be a leader

Learn to accept responsibility

Learn to delegate

People do not grow old; when they cease to grow, they become old.

By   Emerson

Discipline your mind. Discipline yourself.

Never deprive someone of hope; it might be
all they have

Genius is one percent inspiration and ninety-nine percent perspiration
By Thomas Edison

If your ship has not come in, swim out to it. Take action. Create an opportunity for yourself.

People don't plan to fail, they fail to plan

Make sure you are RIGHT, then go ahead

Believe in yourself. No matter how many times you have been knocked down, get up one more time.

Stretch yourself by continuing to expand
your mind and goals

Learn how to sell and market yourself. To sell your ideas you need to sell yourself. To sell your products you need to sell yourself.

Develop your vocabulary

Learn to write a good paragraph. Pick any topic and write a 150 word paragraph. Do this over and over at least once a week for 6 months. This will train your mind and give you excellent experience. It will also build your confidence.

Get plenty of rest and sleep

It may take a lifetime to build a reputation which you could lose in minutes. Therefore control yourself.

Praise in public. Criticize in private.

Learn how to read and understand a financial report

Learn how to gather information. Learn how to understand the facts to make the right decision.

Learn how to interview. Interviewing is a valuable skill that you will be able to use in many areas of your life.

To believe with certainty we must begin
with doubting.
Polish Proverb

Better to bend than to break

Learn to forgive others if you want to be forgiven

Be empathetic. Try to see things from other people's points of view.

Don't spread yourself too thin. Learn to say
no.

It's okay to cry.

VOTE. It is very important that you vote. Vote in the primaries. Vote in the general elections. VOTE. But always study the candidates and the issues before you VOTE.

The reason some men do not succeed is because their wishbone is where their backbone ought to be.

I think luck is the sense to recognize an opportunity and the ability to take advantage of it. Everyone has bad breaks, but everyone has opportunities.

The man who can smile at his breaks and grab his chances gets on.
By Samuel Goldwyn

You decide what is important. You decide your values. You decide your standards. You decide your friends.

Be good and kind to animals ---- especially strays. Feed and pet them. If it is possible go to an animal shelter and ADOPT a dog. A dog will give you unconditional love and friendship.

Love your family. Give them all the love
and support you can.

To have a friend you must be a friend. True friends are priceless.

Your INTEGRITY represents what you are.

If something sounds too good to be true, it probably is.

Learn the rules before you play. That applies to any and all situations in life.

Don't let the fear of striking out get in the
way of your success.
By Babe Ruth

Thomas Edison discovered over 1000 ways that didn't work until he came up with the light bulb

Make the effort to send a card to a
WOUNDED WARRIOR. Try to visit a
hospital full of WOUNDED
WARRIORS. They will appreciate your
visit and cards and you will appreciate their
sacrifice for our country.

Charity is important. If you are able to give ---- someone is in need of your donation .---- may even be dependent upon it.

Expect the unexpected

It is characteristic of wisdom not to do desperate things.
By Henry David Thoreau

Never underestimate anyone

Learn to NEGOTIATE. Role play with your friends until you become very good at it. It is a skill you will use the rest of your life.

Right is right, even if everyone is against it; wrong is wrong, even if everyone is for it.
By William Penn

The best things in life are appreciated most often after they have been lost.

Don't be deceived by first impressions.

Resist temptation

The only man who never makes a mistake is
the man who never does anything.
By Theodore Roosevelt

If it is the TRUTH what does it matter who says it.

Purpose is a source of energy and direction. Discover what moves you. What are your goals? Your reason for getting up in the morning.

You do not need to re-invent the wheel. Research to see if a wheel has been built. Learn from history, learn from others.

Your true happiness may come from helping others.

Always read all contracts thoroughly including the fine print. Never take a salesperson's word on what the contract says. If you want to sign a contract take the time to know what you are signing.

Learn statistics and numbers. When reading about statistics and numbers in newspapers or other print medium, be careful and try to understand what is really said. Be aware of the writer's bias. Statistics can be easily manipulated, misleading.

Read the biographies of highly successful people. Several suggestions are:

George Washington, Abraham Lincoln, Mahatma Gandhi, Winston Churchill, Albert Einstein, Wolfgang Mozart, Walt Disney, Pablo Picasso, and Ronald Reagan.

Don't ever become addicted to anything.

Never be rushed into making an important decision.

Thinking is one thing no one has ever been able to tax.
By Charles Franklin Kettering

Don't count your chickens before they hatch

You don't have a sale until the check clears the bank.

Don't put off for tomorrow what you can do today

Establish priorities in your life ---- with your family, your friends, your time, and with your money.

Educators should be chosen not merely for their special qualifications, but more for their personality and their character, because we teach more by what we are than by what we teach.
By Will Durant

Learn to make the best of any situation

Inspiration ---- Golda Meir was a grandmother before she was Prime Minister of Israel.

Look at every RAINBOW

Self-image ---- YOU are as good as anyone else. Forget and replace any negative programming with POSITIVE thoughts, images, dreams,
and visualizations. Everyday do positive thinking in every realm of your life. Time, hard work and belief in yourself will overcome all obstacles.

Behold the turtle, he makes progress ONLY
when he sticks his neck out.

Communication is vital/important in your personal world. Relationships are based on communication, trust and feelings.

Lost time is never found
By Benjamin Franklin

Learn to stay calm under pressure. Learn to stay in control under pressure.

Inspiration ---- Michelangelo started painting his masterpieces on the ceiling of the Saint Peters Church at age 71. It took over 10 years to paint!

How do you want to be remembered?   For good? For evil?

All the strength and force of man comes from his faith in things unseen. He who believes is strong; he who doubts is weak. Strong convictions precede great actions.

Common sense is the knack of seeing things as they are, and doing things as they ought to be done.

The object of living is work, experience, and happiness. There is joy in work. There is no happiness except in the realization that we have accomplished something.
By Henry Ford

A thing is important if anyone THINKS it important.

Public opinion is a weak tyrant compared with our own private opinion. What a man thinks of himself, that it is which determines, or rather indicates, his fate.

Your mind responds to what you allow to enter it. GARBAGE IN, GARBAGE OUT. BE CAREFUL.

Let us have faith that right makes might, and in that faith let us to the end dare to do our duty as we understand it.
By Abraham Lincoln

In matters of principle, stand like a rock; in matters of taste, swim with the current.
By Thomas Jefferson

Learn to compromise. Half of something may be better than 100% of nothing. But never compromise your principles.

Never do anything against conscience even
if the state/ country demands it.
By Albert Einstein

God's gift to us is life. Our gift to God is what we become. God measures our success in what values/ standards we have and not how much money we have acquired.

The author hopes that the ideas have been helpful. Instead of writing 200 pages on why the Democratic Party and the Republican Party have not governed according to the Constitution of the United States of America, and have NOT represented "We The People" but mainly their self interests, it would have been pages and pages of how these two political parties have gotten America into the mess we presently are in.

The Supreme Court and the U.S. Constitution

The following pages are VERY IMPORTANT.

The author has been working with a CONSTITUTIONAL ATTORNEY who has provided his insights, experiences, and knowledge, to this section of the book. His name is Vernon Steerman.

Attorney Steerman has had valuable experience as a MILITARY lawyer, a FEDERAL lawyer, and a COUNTY lawyer. He has tried numerous law cases in the Kansas Supreme Court. His over 50 years experience with the law makes Steerman a very credible individual to address the following issues.

The main issues that will be addressed are the First Amendment, the Fourteenth Amendment, the Tenth Amendment, and the Thirteenth Amendment.

POSSIBLY and PROBABLY for the first time YOU, the reader, will be a witness to a NEW REVELATION!

IT APPEARS THE FOURTEENTH AMEND-MENT IS UNCONSTITUTIONAL!

THE AUTHOR WANTS TO MAKE IT CLEAR IT IS NOT WHAT IS IN THE FOURTEENTH AMENDMENT OR THIRTEENTH AMENDMENT BUT THE PROCESS OF HOW THEY WERE RATIFIED WAS FLAWED. ESPECIALLY AS OHIO AND NEW JERSEY FINALLY RATIFIED THE FOURTEENTH AMENDMENT IN 2003! THEY OBVIOUSLY THOUGHT THEY HAD NOT RATIFIED.

Writing PURELY FROM A LEGAL POINT OF VIEW, this also means the Thirteenth Amendment is UNCONSTITUTIONAL. We agree with the purpose of the Thirteenth Amendment.

Yes, the Fourteenth Amendment, which is considered the "DUE PROCESS CLAUSE AMENDMENT" which has been the basis for many decisions rendered by the United States Supreme Court, is flawed. The Fourteenth Amendment has been the major legislation which has weakened the Tenth Amendment.

Constitutional attorney Steerman makes a strong case why the Supreme Court has failed the American people.

For example, YOU want to join a social club. A man tells YOU that YOU have to vote for him to be president of the social club. YOU are asked to vote for him before YOU join. YOUR vote is counted as if YOU are a member of the social club. Then YOU become a member. This is what happened to get the Fourteenth Amendment ratified.

But only worst than that.

The facts are that there were 37 states. It took 28 states to ratify the Fourteenth Amendment. Actually only 26 states ratified it, because Ohio and New Jersey rescinded ratification before there were 28 states that ratified it by July 9th, 1868. But the federal Secretary of State, William Seward, certified that the Fourteenth Amendment was ratified and had become part of the Constitution on July 9, 1868. Secretary Steward had no authority under the Constitution to certify that Ohio and New Jersey had ratified the Amendment, as the two states had deratified. Ohio and New Jersey have state rights which cannot and could not have been changed by any federal official. The state legislatures in each state has the authority not the federal government.

The only Confederate state to ratify the Fourteenth Amendment was Tennessee. Therefore, the passage of the Reconstruction Acts prompted Congress to pass a law on March 2, 1867, requiring that a former Confederate state must ratify the Fourteenth Amendment before "said state shall be declared entitled to representation in Congress".

Another amazing fact is that Ohio and New Jersey DID NOT RATIFY THE FOURTEENTH AMENDMENT UNTIL MARCH 12, 2003 AND APRIL 23, 2003 RESPECTIVELY.

SO MUCH FOR NOT HAVING REPRESEN-TATION IN CONGRESS.

Simply based is that it requires three-fourths of all STATES to adopt a Congressional Proposed Amendment. When the Thirteenth and Fourteenth Amendments were ratified on December 6, 1865 and July 9, 1868 the once Confederate States were NOT then LEGAL STATES due to having departed the UNION and NOT readmitted until a "Condition Precedent" each adopted said Amendments. Did the UNION not say that ALL OF THE Confederate States had to adopt the Thirteenth and Fourteenth Amendments in order to be recognized as being a part of the UNION? As the southern States formed a Confederate Union in theory ALL had to ratify the Amendments in order to be rejoined to the Union.

The legal issue: If not a legal STATE of the union how could they legally VOTE and or be coerced to do so? THEY HAD NO DUE PROCESS! This is a most critical issue since the 13th and 14th Amendments have been touted by the U.S. Supreme Court as the DUE PROCESS Amendment. The result being by incorporation by Federal Courts, it transcends ---- rules the Constitution and the Bill of Rights encompassed within the original TEN.

Even more critical the 14th Amendment nullifies the 10th Amendment which created a "REPUBLIC" form of government it being intended , to be, "a strong Federal Government" but, with quasi Sovereign States. The Tenth Amendment states, "The powers not delegated to the United States by the Constitution, nor prohibited by it to the States, are reserved to the States respectively, or to the people."

The first significant Supreme Court case affecting the 1st and 14th Amendments was the "Pierce vs. Society of Sisters", decided on June 1, 1925.

Background: After World War I, some states concerned about the influence of immigrants and "foreign" values looked to public schools for help.

The states drafted laws designed to use schools to promote a common American culture. Oregon passed the Compulsory Education Act which required children to attend public schools. This Act was intended to eliminate all private schools, including Catholic schools. The Sisters of the Holy Names of Jesus and Mary sued the governor, Mr. Pierce, and the state of Oregon. They were concerned about their First Amendment rights. But the Supreme Court added another case, the Hill Military Academy case, which were primarily concerned with their survival. For some reason this became the focal point of the Supreme Court's thinking instead of the original intent of the "Sisters" case. The case then became diluted as the Fourteenth Amendment became the final argument.

From 1789 to 1925, a 136 years, this is the first time that the Supreme Court started to attack the First Amendment and religious freedom. In "Pierce vs. Society of Sisters", the Federal Courts "Monkey See Monkey Do" referenced the reliance on the 14th Amendment was the de facto basis for JUDICIAL ACTIVISM" WHERE INDIVIDUAL RIGHTS AND PROTECTIONS TRAN-SCENDED THEIR "RESPONSIBILITIES " TO BE LAW ABIDING CHRISTIAN VIRTUE BASED ENDOWED CITIZENS CONTRIBUT-ING TO HEALTH AND WELL BEING OF THEIR NATION". Pandora's Box thereafter unsealed creating a Godless (freedom from religion) and lawless land (criminals rights exceeding those victimized). This prelude reference the 14th Amendment deemest vital to setting the stage for subjectively addressing and comprehending the basis for a Nation's transition to Godlessness.

The "Pierce vs. Society of Sisters" case was the beginning of a more liberal interpretation of "Due Process". Thereafter followed some 100 Supreme Court cases and more than 70 Court of Appeals cases reciting it as "Precedence", a legal basis to adopt the premise thereafter, decided therein.

Case #2 ---- Gitlow vs. New York, decided June 8, 1925. This case was decided just 7 days after the "Pierce vs. Society of Sisters case."

This was a decision by the U.S. Supreme Court which ruled that the Fourteenth Amendment to the United States had extended the reach of certain limitations on federal government authority set forth in the First Amendment --- specifically the provisions protecting freedom of speech and freedom of the press --- to the governments of the individual states. It was one of a series of Supreme Court cases that defined the scope of the First Amendment's protection of free speech and established the standard to which a state or the federal government would be held when it criminalized speech or writing.

In the author's opinion this case is a very important case that should have had more influence on following cases that the Supreme Court decided.

Background: In the years following the Red Scare of 1919 -20, a variety of leftists, either anarchists, sympathizers with the Bolshevik, labor activists, or members of a communist or socialist party, were convicted for violating the Espionage Act of 1917 and Sedition Act of 1918 on the basis of their writings or statements. Benjamin Gitlow, a member of the Socialist Party of America who had served in the New York State Assembly, was charged with criminal anarchy under New York's Criminal Anarchy Law of 1902 for publishing in July 1919 a document called, "Left Wing Manifesto" in the Revolutionary Age, a newspaper for which he served as business manager. He was convicted. New York's Criminal Anarchy Law was passed in 1902 following the assassination of President of the United States William McKinley by an anarchist in Buffalo, New York, in September 1901.

The Court had to consider whether it could review a challenge to a state law on the basis that it violated the federal constitution. If it determined that such a challenge lay within the scope of its authority, then it had to review the application of the law to the case at hand, the specific violation of the stature. It upheld Gitlow's conviction.

The Supreme Court previously held, in Barron vs. Baltimore (1833), that the Constitution's Bill of Rights applied only to the federal government, that states were free to enforce statures that restricted the rights enumerated in the Bill of Rights, and that the federal courts could not interfere with the enforcement of such statures. Gitlow vs. New York partly reversed that precedent and began a trend toward its nearly complete reversal. The Supreme Court now holds that almost every provision of the Bill of Rights applies to both the federal government and the states.

The Supreme Court relied on the "due process clause" of the Fourteenth Amendment, which prohibits a state from depriving "any person of life, liberty, or property, without due process of law." The Court stated that "For present purposes we may and do assume that the rights of freedom of speech and freedom of the press were among the fundamental personal rights and liberties protected by the due process clause of the Fourteenth Amendment from impairment by the states."

The Court used the doctrine first enunciated in Gitlow v New York in other cases, such as De Jorge vs. Oregon (1937), Wolf vs. Colorado (1949), and Gideon vs. Wainwright (1963), to extend the reach of the Bill of Rights. Constitutional scholars refer to this as the "incorporation doctrine," meaning that the Supreme Court has identified rights specified in the Bill of Rights and incorporated them into the liberties covered by the due process clause of the Fourteenth Amendment.

FREE SPEECH ---- THE SUPREME COURT UPHELD GITLOW'S CONVICTION ON THE BASIS THAT THE GOVERNMENT MAY SUPPRESS OR PUNISH SPEECH THAT DIRECTLY ADVOCATES THE UNLAWFUL OVER-THROW OF THE GOVERNMENT AND IT UPHELD THE CONSTITUTIONALITY OF THE STATE STATUE AT ISSUE, WHICH MADE IT A CRIME TO ADVOCATE THE DUTY, NEED, OR APPROPRIATENESS OF OVERTHROWING GOVERNMENT BY FORCE OR VIOLENCE.

Justice Edward Terry Sanford's majority opinion attempted to define more clearly the "clear and present danger" test developed a few years earlier in Schenck vs. United States (1919). He embraced "the bad tendency test" found in Abrams vs. United States (1919), which held that a "State may punish utterances endangering the foundations of government and threatening its overthrow by unlawful means" because such speech clearly "presents a sufficient danger to the public peace and to the security of the State". According to Sanford, a "single revolutionary spark may kindle a fire that, smoldering for a time, may burst into a sweeping and destructive conflagration."

Case #3 ---- Cantwell vs. Connecticut decided 1940.

This was a Supreme Court decision that incorporated or applied to the states, through the Due Process Clause of the Fourteenth Amendment, the First Amendment's protection of religious free exercise.

Before the Cantwell decision, it was not legally clear that the First Amendment protected religious practitioners at the state and local levels as well as federal. But the Supreme Court in Cantwell said it did.

The Court found that Cantwell was protected by the First and Fourteenth Amendments. This case incorporated the First Amendment's Free Exercise Clause, thereby applying free exercise from intrusive state action.

Case #4 ----Everson vs. Board of Education, decided February 10, 1947

This was a landmark decision of the Supreme Court which applied the Establishment Claus of the First Amendment as binding upon the states through the Due Process Clause of the

Fourteenth Amendment. The decision in Everson marked a turning point in the interpretation and application of disestablishment law in the modern era.

A landmark decision which applied the First Amendment, Reference the federal government cannot establish religion to states via 14th Amendment Due Process Amendment. Wherein established by a 5-4 decision. "Neither a state or the federal government can set-up or prefer one religion over another." In the now famous letter by Thomas Jefferson to a friend where the U.S. Supreme Court took only a part of Jefferson's letter to make a case, "a wall of separation between church and state".

Everson lost the case. The supporters of religion won the case, won the battle. But they ended up losing the war as for some reason Justice Hugo Black issued a broad interpretation of the Establishment Clause that became the guide the Court used for decisions for decades to come.

"The 'establishment of religion' clause of the First Amendment means at least this: Neither a state nor the Federal Government can set up a church. Neither can pass laws which aid one religion, aid all religions or prefer one religion over another. Neither can force nor influence a person to go to or to remain away from church against his will or force him to profess a belief or disbelief in any religion. No person can be punished or professing religious beliefs or disbeliefs, for church attendance or non-attendance. No tax in any amount, large or small, can be levied to support any religious activities or institutions, whatever they may be called, or whatever form they may adopt to teach or practice religion. Neither a state nor the Federal Government can, openly or secretly, participate in the affairs of any religious organizations or groups and vice versa. In the words of Jefferson, the clause against establishment of religion by law was intended 'to erect a wall of separation between Church and State.'"

Case #5 ---- McCollum vs. Board of Education, decided March 8, 1948.

Ruled the use of public school facilities by religious organizations to give instruction to school children VIOLATES the First Amendment "Establishment Clause."

Case #6 ---- Lorach et al vs. Clauson et al, decided April 28, 1952.

Decision reference school district which allowing students to receive religious instruction are acceptable if "Instruction takes place away from school campus for one hour per week without school funding."

Case #7 ---- Steven I. Engel et al vs. V. William J. Vitale et al, decided June 25, 1962.

Unconstitutional for state officials to compose an official school prayer and encourage its recitation in public schools. Prayer questioned:

Almighty God, we acknowledge our dependence upon Thee, and we beg thy blessings upon us, our parents, our teachers, and our county. Amen."

This followed by subsequent decisions reference government directed prayers in schools. Cases ---- Wallace vs. Jaffee (1985), Lee vs. Weisman (1992), and Santa Fe ISD vs. Doe (2006). extended to ban school organized student prayer at high school football games.

Case #8 ---- Abingon School District vs. Schempe, decided June 17, 1963.

Held: School sponsored Bible reading in public schools in the United States to be unconstitutional.

Case #9 ---- Flast vs. Cohen, decide 1968.

Held: A taxpayer has "standing" ,(entitlement), to sue the government to prevent unconstitutional use of taxpayer funds reference support of religion.

This raises the question why a taxpayer does not have "standing" to sue the government when it created and fostered "social welfare".

Case #10 ---- Epperson vs. Arkansas decided in 1968.

Held: First Amendment prohibits a state from requiring teaching and learning must be tailored to principles or prohibitions of and religious sect or dogma, i.e., teaching of creation science alongside evolution.

Chief Justice Earl Warren said, "The constitution means what the Supreme Court says it means".

Case #11 ---- Bob Jones University vs. United States, decided May 24, 1984.

Held: IRS could revoke tax exempt status per 501 (C3) whose practices were contrary to government public policy, reference eradicating racial discrimination. Facts of case: entailed inter-racial married and or dating being excluded from enrollment. Reference Civil rights Act of 1964.

Case #12 ---- Marsh vs. Chambers, decided June 5, 1983.

Held: Nebraska hiring of a state paid chaplain to open legislative sessions DID NOT violate the First Amendment Establishment clause because of its "unique history."

Due Process Clause

The Due Process Clause of the Fourteenth Amendment applies against only the states, but it is otherwise textually identical to the Due Process Clause of the Fifth Amendment, which applies against the federal government; both clauses have been interpreted to encompass identical doctrines of procedural due process and substantive due process. Procedural due process is the guarantee of a fair legal process when the government seeks to burden a person's protected interests in life, or property, and substantive due process is the guarantee that the fundamental rights of citizens will not be encroached on by government. The Due Process Clause of the Fourteenth Amendment also incorporates most of the provisions in the Bill of Rights, which were originally applied against only the federal government, and applies them against the states.

Substantive Due Process

Beginning with Allgeyer vs. Louisiana (1797), the Court interpreted the Due Process Clause as providing substantive protection to private contracts, thus prohibiting a variety of social and economic regulation; this principle was referred to as "freedom of contract". Thus the Court struck down a law decreeing maximum hours for workers in a bakery in Lochner vs. New York (1905), and struck down a minimum wage law in Adkins vs. Children's Hospital (1923). In Meyer vs. Nebraska (1923), the Court stated that the "liberty" protected by the Due Process Clause, "without doubt denotes not merely freedom from bodily restraint but also the right of the individual to contract, to engage in any of the common occupations of life, to acquire useful knowledge, to marry, establish a home and bring up children, to worship God according to the dictates of his conscience, and generally to enjoy those privileges long recognized at common law to the orderly pursuit of happiness by free men."

However, the Court did uphold some economic regulation, such as state Prohibition laws (Mugler vs. Kansas, (1887), laws declaring maximum hours for mine workers (Holden vs. Hrdy, (1898), laws declaring maximum hours for female workers (Muller vs. Oregon, (1908), and President Woodrow Wilson's intervention in a railroad strike

(Wilson vs. New, (1917), as well as federal laws regulating narcotics (United States vs. Doremus, (1919). The Court repudiated, but did not explicitly overrule, the "freedom of contract" line of cases in (West Coast Hotel vs. Parrish, (1937).

Although the "freedom of contract" has fallen into disfavor, by the 1960s, the Court extended its interpretation of substantive due process to INCLUDE OTHER RIGHTS AND FREEDOMS THAT ARE NOT ENUMERATED IN THE CONSTITUTION BUT THAT, ACCORDING TO THE COURT, EXTEND OR DERIVE FROM EXISTING RIGHTS. FOR EXAMPLE, THE DUE PROCESS CLAUSE IS ALSO THE FOUNDATION OF A CONSTITUTIONAL RIGHT TO PRIVACY. The court first ruled that privacy was protected by the Constitution in Griswold vs. Connecticut (1965), which overturned Connecticut law criminalizing birth control. While Justice William O. Douglas wrote for the majority that the right to privacy was found in the "penumbras" of various provisions in the Bill of Rights, Justices Arthur Goldberg and John Marshall Harlan II wrote in concurring opinions that the "liberty" protected by the Due Process Clause included individual privacy.

Merriam-Webster Dictionary defines "penumbras" as:

1. A space of partial illumination (as in an eclipse) between the perfect shadow on all sides and full light. A shaded region surrounding the dark central portion of a sunspot.

2. A surrounding or adjoining region in which something exists in a lesser degree: fringe.

Justice William O. Douglas what does that have to do with birth control?

The right to privacy was the basis for Roe vs. Wade (1973), in which the court invalidated a Texas law forbidding abortion except to save the mother's health. Like Goldberg and Harlan's concurring opinions in Grisvold, the majority opinion authored by Justice Harry A, Blackmun located the right to privacy in the Due Process Clause's protection of liberty. The decision disallowed many state and federal abortion restrictions, and it became one of the most controversial in the Court's history. In Planned Parenthood vs. Casey (1992), the Court decided that "the essential holding of Roe vs. Wade should be retained and once again reaffirmed. In Lawrence vs. Texas (2003), the Court found that a state law against same-sex sexual intercourse violated the right to privacy.

Procedural Due Process

When the government seeks to burden a person's protected liberty interest or property interest, the Supreme Court has held that procedural due process requires that, at a minimum, the government provide the person notice, an opportunity to be heard at an oral hearing, and a decision by a neutral decision maker. For example, such process is due when a government agency seeks to terminate civil service employees, expel a student from public school, or cut off a welfare recipient 's benefits.

The Court has also ruled the Due Process Clause requires judges to recuse themselves in cases where the judge has a conflict of interest.

The author's comment to the issue of privacy. The Bill of Rights does not mention the word "privacy". But it is not a far stretch that privacy can be inferred in the pursuit of happiness. But as used in the Supreme Court case of Roe vs. Wade it is an inadequate use. Privacy as it relates to what causes an abortion is not proper. If we say what happens in the bedroom or wherever a woman gets pregnant that may be done in privacy, but that action may have an unwanted result. There may be consequences to having sex. If that action results in the woman becoming pregnant that is a normal consequence. When a woman is pregnant she is going to have a baby. BUT THE ACT OF KILLING THE BABY IS NOT AN ACT OF PRIVACY, BUT AN ACT OF KILLING THE BABY IS A ACT OF KILLING THE BABY. IT HAS NOTHING TO DO WITH PRIVACY. NO MATTER WHERE THE KILLING TAKES PLACE ITS STILL KILLING. THE SUPREME COURT JUSTICES WHO VOTED FOR THE RIGHT OF A WOMAN TO KILL THEIR BABY WILL FACE THEIR CONSEQUENCES ON THE JUDGMENT DAY. OVER 50 MILLION BABIES HAVE BEEN KILLED IN THE UNITED STATES SINCE THESE JUDGES APPROVED KILLING OF BABIES.

The TEN COMMANDMENTS ARE CLEAR, "THOU SHALT NOT KILL". Therefore, besides the judges who voted for the killing of a baby, we can also add any politician who has voted for or defended Roe vs. Wade. One day they will answer to God.

Case #13 ---- Arizona Christian School vs. Winn, decided April 4, 2010

Held: Taxpayer "lacked Standing (to sue) under Article 3, because they are challenging a "tax code", rather than government "spending".

Case #14 ---- Texas Monthly Inc. vs. Bullock, decided Feb 21, 1989.

Issue: Texas exempted Sales Tax for a religious publication.

Held: Unconstitutional. By confining tax exemption exclusively to sale of religious publications, Texas provided preferential support for the communication of religious messages.

Case #15 ---- County of Allegheny vs. American Civil Liberties Union, decided July 3, 1989

Held: County of Allegheny violated the "Establish Clause" by displaying a "crèche" (a set of statues that represent the scene of Jesus Christ's birth and that is displayed during Christmas) in the County Courthouse. "It advanced religion".

Case #16 ---- Town of Greece, New York vs. Galloway, decided on May 5, 2014.

Held: Town of Greece DOES NOT violate First Amendment' Establishment Clause by opening its legislature sessions with prayer.

Case #17 ---- McCoy County vs. ACLU, decided June 27, 2005.

Held: Displaying Ten Commandments on

government property was unconstitutional.

On same day another decision but different outcome.

Case #18 ---- Van Orden vs. Perry, decided June 27, 2005.

Held: Ten Commandments monument erected on grounds of Texas capitol in Austin DID NOT violate Establishment Clause because it conveyed a historic and social meaning rather than an inclusive religious endorsement.

Case #19 ---- Lynch vs. Donnely, decided on March 5, 1984.

Held: Pawtucket, Rhode Island's annual Christmas display in city's shopping district of a Santa Claus house, Christmas Tree, and banner "Season's Greetings" and a crèche since 1943, WAS NOT an effort to advocate a particular religion. It had "Legitimate Secular Purpose"

Case #20 ---- Stone vs. Graham, decided on November 17, 1980.

Held: Kentucky statue posting of a copy of the Ten Commandments purchased with private contributions on the wall of each classroom unconstitutional because it lacks a "Secular Legislative Purpose".

Case #21 ---- Agostini vs. Felton, decided on June 23, 1997.

1965 Title I, Elementary and Secondary Act (adjunct to Civil Rights Act of 1964) with goal of providing adequate education to all children in U.S. regardless of individual economic conditions.

Held: Revised Court of Appeals Court Aguilar vs. Felton (1985) to U.S. Supreme Court. Allowed public school teachers to instruct at religious schools, so long as material was secular and neutral in Nature and no excessive entanglement "between government and religion was apparent.

Case #22 ---- Brown vs. Board of Education of Topeka, decided 1954.

This was a landmark U.S. Supreme Court case which the Court declared state laws establishing separate public schools for black and white students to be unconstitutional. The decision overturned the Plessy vs. Ferguson decision of 1896, which allowed state sponsored segregation, insofar as it applied to public education. As a result, de jure racial segregation was ruled a violation of the Equal Protection Clause of the Fourteenth Amendment. This ruling paved the way for integration.

The First Amendment

By the National Center For Constitutional Studies

The First Amendment was written to prevent the national government, federal government, from establishing a national church. During the colonial days each colony had its own official religion. That means each colony recognized a particular Christian denomination as the official state religion supported by taxpayer dollars.

During those early days each denomination feared that one particular denomination would be crowned the national religion. For instance, the Quakers didn't want the Puritans running the nation, and certainly the Puritans didn't want the Quakers running the nation either. This fear and mistrust led to liberty.

This brings us to the Bill of Rights. As a result of that mistrust and fear the Founders said that, "Congress shall make no law respecting an establishing of religion." That means that the national government, federal government, can't make a law setting up a particular denomination as an official national faith. The amendment also goes on to say that Congress shall make no law prohibiting the free exercise of religion.

Basically the national government, federal government, is to have a hands- off policy on religion, period. The people are free to assemble and to worship as they please.

The First Amendment was the first step toward total religious freedom everywhere. The Constitution didn't forbid the states from establishing religion since they already had established religions.

The Founders knew that a state church, one financed by tax dollars , would become corrupt because it doesn't answer to the people. As a result, it would become an arm of the state, government, and give religious significance to every act of government, even if the acts are unjust. This has been the nature of religion from the days of earliest history.

Freedom of religion means freedom to voice your opinions without fear of punishment. The First Amendment was intended to give people a free voice in speaking up against a power hungry government. In Colonial America many ministers gave election sermons which would point out moral issues facing the day. If the government controlled those ministers, there be no voice against government corruption. After all, you don't bite the hand that feeds you.

We need to restore the First Amendment in America as it was meant to be by our Founding Fathers.

FROM THE BIBLE
JEREMIAH CHAPTER 18:7-10

Verse 7

At what instant I shall speak concerning a nation, and concerning a kingdom, to pluck up, and to pull down, and to destroy it;

Verse 8

If that nation, against whom I have pronounced, turn from their evil, I will repent of the evil that I thought to do unto them.

Verse 9

And at what instant I shall speak concerning a nation, and concerning a kingdom, to build and to plant it;

Verse 10

If it do evil in my sight, that it obey not my voice, then I will repent of the good, wherewith I said I would benefit them.

Verse 11

Thus saith the Lord; Behold, I frame evil against you, and devise a device against you; return ye now everyone from his evil way, and make your ways and your doings good.

Added this for the people who do not have their own copy of the Constitution.

Five Amendments were mentioned in this book. The First, the Fifth, the Tenth, the Thirteen, and the Fourteenth.

The First Amendment

Congress shall make no law respecting an establishment of religion, or prohibiting the free exercise thereof, or abridging the freedom of speech, or of the press, or the right of the people peaceably to assemble, and to petition the Government for a redress of grievances.

The Fifth Amendment

No person shall be held to answer for a capital, or otherwise infamous crime, unless on a presentment or indictment of a Grand Jury, except in cases arising in the land or naval forces, or in the Militia, when in actual service in time of War or public danger; nor shall any person be subject for the same offence to be twice put in jeopardy of life or limb; nor shall be compelled in any criminal case to be a witness against himself, nor be deprived of life, liberty, or property, without due process of law; nor shall private property be taken for public use, without just compensation.

The Tenth Amendment

The powers not delegated to the United States by the Constitution, nor prohibited by it to the States, are reserved to the States respectively, or to the people.

The Thirteenth Amendment

Section 1. Neither slavery nor involuntary servitude, except as a punishment for crime whereof the party shall have been duly convicted, shall exist within the United States, or any place subject to their jurisdiction.

Section 2. Congress shall have power to enforce this article by appropriate legislation.

The Fourteenth Amendment

Section 1. All persons born or naturalized in the United States and subject to the jurisdiction thereof, are citizens of the United States and of the State wherein they reside. No State shall make or enforce any law which shall abridge the privileges or immunities of citizens of the United States; nor shall any State deprive any person of life, liberty, or property, without due process of law; nor deny to any person within its jurisdiction the equal protection of the laws.

Section 2. Representatives shall be apportioned among the several States according to their respective numbers, counting the whole number of persons in each state, excluding Indians not taxed. But when the right to vote at any election for the choice of electors for President and Vice President of the United States, Representatives in Congress, the Executive and Judicial officers of a State, or the members of the Legislature thereof, is denied to any of the male inhabitants of such State, being twenty-one years of age, and citizens of the United States, or in any way abridged, except for participation in rebellion, or other crime, the basis of representation therein shall be reduced in the proportion which the number of such male citizens shall bear to the whole number of male citizens twenty-one of age in such State.

Section 3. No person shall be a Senator or Representative in Congress, or elector of President and Vice President, or hold any office, civil or military, under the United States, or under any

State, who, having previously taken an oath, as a member of Congress, or as an officer of the United States, or as a member of any State legislature, or as an executive or judicial officer of any State, to support the Constitution of the United States, shall have engaged in insurrection or rebellion against the same, or given aid or comfort to the enemies thereof. But Congress may by a vote of two-thirds of each House, remove such disability.

Section 4. The validity of the public debt of the United States, authorized by law, including debts incurred for payment of pensions and bounties for services in suppressing insurrection or rebellion, shall not be questioned. But neither the United States nor any State shall assume or pay any debt or obligation incurred in aid of insurrection or rebellion against the United States, or any claim for the loss or emancipation of any slave; but all such debts, obligations and claims shall be held illegal and void.

Section 5. The Congress shall have power to enforce, by appropriate legislation, the provisions of this article.

ACKNOWLEDGEMENTS

The author thanks Vernon Steerman for his support and contributions of the court cases. The author acknowledges the use of Wikipedia, especially for the court cases.

FINAL
THOUGHTS
(Taken from an article by Jim Bramlett)

W e would like to think of the U.S. Supreme Court as a fountainhead of truth, where wise men and women deliberate (hopefully prayerfully) and flawlessly rule on the intent of the Constitution.

If that were true, there would be an ongoing consistency in their decisions. Unfortunately, that has been far from reality. For example, for most of our country's history, the Justices recognized that they were subject to a higher law found in God's Word. The Court viewed law as President Calvin Coolidge did when he declared, "Men do not make laws, they do but discover them. Laws must be justified by something more than the will of the majority. They must rest upon the eternal foundations of righteousness."

Here are a few of the historic cases that reaffirmed Biblical principles:

- Vidal vs. Girard's Executors (1844): The Court produced a ruling which said, "Christianity is not to be maliciously and openly reviled and blasphemed against, to the annoyance of believers or the injury of the public." The Court's decision asked the question, "Where can the purest principles of morality be learned so clearly or so perfectly as from the New Testament?"

- Holy Trinity vs. United States (1892) : The Supreme Court cited document after document from American history and concluded, "There is no dissonance in these declarations. There is a universal language pervading them all, having one meaning; they affirm and reaffirm that this is a religious nation." The ruling states bluntly, "This is a Christian nation."

- United States vs. Macintosh (1931): The Supreme Court declared, "We are a Christian people according to one another the equal right of religious freedom, and acknowledging with reverence the duty of obedience to God."

IN CONCLUSION — AUTHOR'S THOUGHTS

In the important Supreme Court case of 1892 (Holy Trinity vs. United States), the legal scholar and Supreme Court Justice, David Brewer, stated," If we examine the Constitutions of the various States, we find in them a constant recognition of religious obligations. Every constitution of every one of the forty-four States, contains language which either directly or by clear implication, recognizes a profound reverence for religion and an assumption that its influence in all human affairs is essential to the well-being of the community."

Justice Brewer said, "There is no dissonance in these declarations. There is a universal language pervading them all, having one meaning; they affirm and reaffirm that this is a religious nation. These are not individual sayings, declarations of private persons; they are organic utterances; they speak the voice of the entire people."

www.ingramcontent.com/pod-product-compliance
Lightning Source LLC
Chambersburg PA
CBHW070631290526
45790CB00001B/74